COSTUME AROUND THE WORLD
Spain

Kathy Elgin

CHELSEA CLUBHOUSE
An Imprint of Chelsea House Publishers

Copyright © 2008 Bailey Publishing Associates Ltd

Produced for Chelsea Clubhouse by Bailey Publishing Associates Ltd
11a Woodlands, Hove BN3 6TJ
England

Project Manager: Roberta Bailey
Editor: Alex Woolf
Text Designer: Jane Hawkins
Picture Research: Roberta Bailey and Shelley Noronha

Chelsea Clubhouse
An imprint of Chelsea House Publishers
132 West 31st Street
New York NY 10001

ISBN 978-0-7910-9772-4

Library of Congress Cataloging-in-Publication Data
Costume around the world.—1st ed.
    v. cm.
    Includes bibliographical references and index.
    Contents: [1] China / Anne Rooney—[2] France / Kathy Elgin—[3] Germany / Cath Senker—[4] India / Kathy Elgin—[5] Italy / Kathy Elgin—[6] Japan / Jane Bingham—[7] Mexico / Jane Bingham—[8] Saudi Arabia / Cath Senker—[9] Spain / Kathy Elgin—[10] United States / Liz Gogerly.
    ISBN 978-0-7910-9765-6 (v. 1)—ISBN 978-0-7910-9766-3 (v. 2)—ISBN 978-0-7910-9767-0 (v. 3)—ISBN 978-0-7910-9768-7 (v. 4)—ISBN 978-0-7910-9769-4 (v. 5)—ISBN 978-0-7910-9770-0 (v. 6)—ISBN 978-0-7910-9771-7 (v. 7)—ISBN 978-0-7910-9773-1 (v. 8)— ISBN 978-0-7910-9772-4 (v. 9)—ISBN 978-0-7910-9774-8 (v. 10) 1. Clothing and dress—Juvenile literature.
    GT518.C67 2008
    391—dc22   2007042756

Printed and bound in Hong Kong

10 9 8 7 6 5 4 3 2 1

The publishers would like to thank the following for permission to reproduce their pictures:
Chris Fairclough Worldwide Ltd: 9 (Ed Parker), 19.
Rex Features: 11 (Mark Baynes), 20 (Sipa Press), 27 (Richard Sowersby).
Topfoto: 4, 5, 6, 7, 8 (Prisma/VWPics), 10, 12, 13 (Nano Calvo), 14 (Prisma-VW), 15 (Hilary Shedel-Arena Images), 16, 17 (Larry Mangino/Image Works), 18 (Benoit Roland/Image Works), 21 (National News), 22 (Roger-Viollet), 23, 24, 25 (Caro), 26 and title page, 28, 29.

Contents

Mountain, Sea, and Pasture

Spain is cut off from Europe to the north by the Pyrenees Mountains, which form a natural barrier. Its people are descendants of the many invaders from the south, including Greeks, Romans, and Jews. The most influential settlers, however, were the Moors. They were Muslim Arabs from North Africa who ruled the country until the late 15th century.

A united kingdom

Spain has had a turbulent history. It has only been a united country since the end of the 15th century. It still has strong regional divisions, each with its own costume, food, and languages. The Basque country and Catalonia in the north and Andalusia in the south are especially proud of their regional identity. The dictator Francisco Franco (ruled 1939–1975) tried to stamp out these differences. Since his death, there has been a strong revival of regional loyalty.

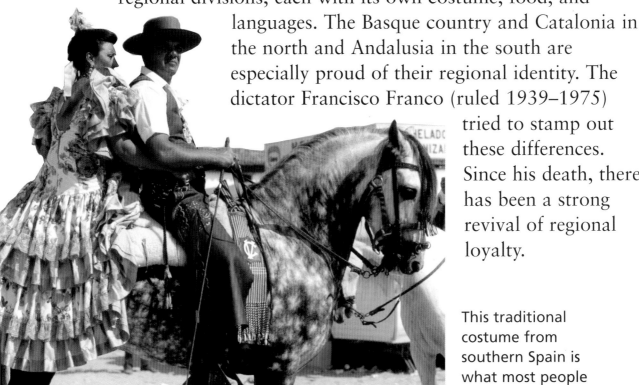

This traditional costume from southern Spain is what most people consider typically Spanish.

Proud people

Spanish people are considered to be proud, passionate, and quick-tempered. They have a reputation for living life to the fullest. They have more holidays than anywhere else in the world, most of which are a good excuse to wear traditional dress.

Today most young people have moved to cities in search of work. They wear the usual stylish international fashions. The older generation, left behind in rural villages, still wears old-fashioned clothes. Parts of Andalusia in the south and Extremadura in the west are very poor.

Local fiestas often feature parades of giant doll heads. Some are storybook characters, while others make fun of politicians.

Don Quixote

Don Quixote, a character in a 17th-century novel by Miguel de Cervantes, represents the Spain of long ago. Don Quixote has read so many old books about chivalry that he thinks he is a gallant knight. He dresses in a homemade suit of armor and treats a local farm girl as a fine lady. In his eyes, her rough country clothes are fine gowns.

Clothes through the Ages

In medieval Spain, some people wore Moorish dress, like their rulers. Others wore the style set by the Burgundian court in France. The Burgundian style was worn all over Europe. Ladies wore long gowns with trailing sleeves and tall, pointed headdresses or veils. Men wore cloaks, belted tunics, and hose.

The golden age

Philip II of Spain (ruled 1556–1598) was the most powerful monarch in the world. All the courts of Europe imitated his style. The fashion was severe but elegant, reflecting the king's gloomy nature. Outfits were entirely of black silk, except for the starched white ruffs around the neck. Men wore tailored doublet and hose, while women wore gowns with farthingales underneath.

The farthingale was a wire frame that made the delicate silk skirt stick out from the waist, as in this famous painting by Velásquez.

Spain continued to dominate European culture through the 1600s. There were great advances in literature, painting, and fashion. Portraits by Diego Velázquez, the court painter, show the royal family and aristocrats wearing very elaborate costumes in rich velvets, silk, and satin. He painted ordinary people too, so we know that they wore simple wool smocks and tunics.

Simpler fashion

By the 18th century, dress had become more relaxed. The portraits of court painter Francisco Goya (1746–1828) show women wearing dresses of muslin and lace with sashes and mantillas (lace shawls). Men wore long wool coats and knee breeches.

In the 19th century, the riding outfit of aristocratic landowners consisted of a bolero jacket, calf-length pants, and boots. This developed into the typical Spanish *caballero* costume worn today.

Maja style

A *majo* or *maja* was a member of the Madrid artistic scene in the late 18th century. Although *majos* and *majas* were often from a lower class of society, they had great style and exaggerated ways of dressing and behaving. They wore elaborate outfits with colored sashes and mantillas. Their style was much imitated by the upper classes.

The Duchess of Alba, painted here by Goya, loved to dress in the *maja* style.

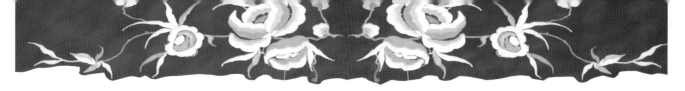

A Rugged Land

Spain is a big country with a varied climate. People speak of the "wet" north and the "dry" south. Many areas also experience extremes of temperature. The Meseta, or high central plateau, has hot, dry summers but can be freezing in winter. Most people here are sheep farmers, and the local clothing is traditionally made of wool.

The sunny coasts

The eastern Mediterranean coast has hot, dry summers and mild winters, which make it a popular tourist destination. The Costa del Sol, with its flat, sandy beaches, has the best weather—an average of 300 days of sunshine per year. Beach vacations and water sports are the main industries.

Fishing

Galicia is wet, with mild winters and cool summers. Along its steep Atlantic coastline, fishermen catch

Fishermen from Galicia wear waterproof overalls and boots as protection from rain and sea.

over half the fish and seafood eaten in Spain. Fishermen's sweaters and traditional sailor costumes worn by little boys recall Spain's seafaring heritage.

Oranges and almonds

Farming remains an important industry in Spain. In the dry, central areas, farmers grow wheat, olives, and vines. Oranges and lemons grow around Valencia, and there are vineyards all over Spain. Dairy cattle live on the lush pastures in the north, providing milk and cheese.

The basin of the Guadalquivir River in Andalusia is the hottest region. Farmworkers growing oranges, olives, and almonds need their loose cotton clothing, hats, and headscarves as protection against the fierce sun. Even the donkeys are given straw hats.

In some parts of Spain, farming has not changed much in centuries.

Wear your oldest clothes!

La Tomatina is one of the most unusual agricultural festivals. It takes place in Buñol, near Valencia. People gather in the town square to pelt each other with tons of ripe tomatoes donated by local growers. Even observers and tourists get splattered! The festival began in 1944 when demonstrators attacked local officials, and has remained popular ever since.

Church and People

Roman Catholicism was Spain's official religion until 1978. Most of the population is still Catholic, but not all go to church regularly. Although religion has less influence today over people's lives, important events such as marriage, christenings, and funerals still take place in church. Nuns and priests in black robes are a common sight on the streets.

People are expected to dress modestly in church. Bare arms, low necklines, and shorts are not permitted. Women always carry a shawl or a scarf to cover their head and shoulders.

Multicultural Spain

In medieval Spain, Christians and Jews lived peacefully alongside the ruling Muslim majority for centuries. When Christians regained control in 1492, they

This painting of a funeral by El Greco includes several religious figures, from a humble monk to bishops wearing elaborate robes.

expelled the Jews that same year and the Muslims in the early 1600s. The fiesta at Alcoi is a friendly reenactment of battles between Moors and Christians with both "armies" wearing traditional dress.

Semana santa

Spain's religious holidays are celebrated with processions and floats. The processions of Holy Week are very dramatic, especially those in Seville. Men who are members of a Catholic brotherhood are called *nazarenos*. They dress in long robes and pointed hoods in purple, black, or white and carry candles. Others, called *penitentes*, wear different hoods and carry heavy crosses. Women in black carry candles. Musicians with drums and trumpets play mournful music. This solemn occasion is followed by the *feria*. Everyone has new clothes and goes to the fair.

Medieval clothing laws

Before the Jews were expelled in 1492, laws were passed to identify and discriminate against them. They had to wear ankle-length robes but could not wear silk or furs. Green and white, the colors of Islam, were forbidden. Their distinctive, cone-shaped hats had to be yellow to distinguish them from Muslim turbans.

The *nazarenos,* with their faces hidden under hoods, can look quite sinister.

An Ancient Textile Tradition

Spain's textile trade is based in Catalonia in the north. It dates to the Moors, who introduced a special breed of sheep called the merino, which has very soft wool. Suits made from merino wool are the best quality and much in demand. The fabric called gabardine dates to the Middle Ages, when *gabardina*, a wool fabric, was used for making cloaks.

Silk and cotton

The secrets of silk manufacture were originally brought from China by Moorish traders. Those who settled in Spain brought mulberry trees with them on which to grow silk worms. Knights returning from the Crusades brought back fine brocades and velvets from the East. The silk industry still flourishes today, especially around Granada,

A silk dress patterned with polka dots is the traditional flamenco costume. The net underskirt is a more modern addition.

12

where scarves and ties are produced. Cotton was grown in Spain, but imports from the American colonies replaced it. Today cheap imports threaten Spain's whole textile industry.

Spanish leather and metalwork

The Moors brought the skill of tanning leather to Córdoba, a city in Andalusia. Spanish leather is famous worldwide, especially for jackets, boots, and shoes. In the 1600s, tons of silver were imported from Spain's American colonies for use in swords, jewelry, and coinage manufactured in Toledo in central Spain. This was combined with Moorish leatherwork skills to produce finely tooled leather belts with silver buckles. These are still produced in the area today.

Lace making

The best Spanish lace comes from Extremadura, La Mancha, and Catalonia. It is handmade by local women who work sitting outside their houses and sell the finished lace to an agent. It is used for mantillas, collars, and church vestments. Traditionally, Spanish wedding rings are presented on a tiny pillow of lace.

Spanish riding boots have pointed toes and high heels. They are decorated with engraved patterns and studs.

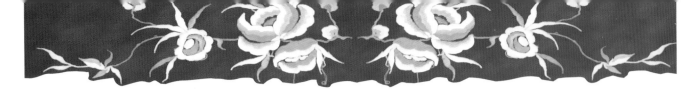

Costumes from the Regions

What we call typical Spanish dress is really the traditional costume of Andalusia. The man's outfit is a short jacket, calf-length pants, riding boots, and a wide-brimmed black hat. Women wear low-necked, tightly fitting dresses with flounces at the knee, and a fringed shawl.

Plain or colorful

Regional costumes often reflect the countryside. Andalusia's costume is colorful, but that of bleak Extremadura is very plain. Costume in Galicia still has a medieval quality, with simple black vests and embroidered white shirts or blouses worn over black pants or skirts.

In the Basque country, men wear either white shirts and pants with a red sash or black knee

Catalonian dancers perform a traditional sardana at a folk festival.

breeches and shoes, white stockings, and a vest. Either way, a Basque beret, the region's official headgear, is essential. Women wear their white blouse and black vest with a long wool skirt in red or green, white stockings, black shoes, and a white headscarf. Colored scarves go around the neck.

The color of life

In costume, colors are important. Red represents love, green is for nature and long life, white for purity, and blue for the heavens. Also, small details reveal a person's social standing and if he or she is married or single.

City slickers

Madrid has its own city costume. The men wear black-and-white-checked jackets, vests, and flat caps with a handkerchief tied around the neck. Women wear elegant frilled dresses, headscarves, and shawls. Boys wear gray suits with piped edges.

Viva flamenco

Flamenco is a style of music and dance that began in Andalusia and blends Moorish, Jewish, and gypsy traditions. Female dancers wear a flounced cotton dress and high heels and have flowers in their hair. Men wear a white shirt and tight, high-waisted black pants, a vest, and Cuban-heeled shoes.

Above: A silk shawl with long fringe gives added grace to the flamenco dancer's movements.

Clothes for Special Occasions

First Communion is a very important occasion in the life of a Catholic child in Spain. For their big day, girls wear white bridal outfits and veils and carry prayer books and flowers. Little boys wear formal suits and bow ties.

The 19th-century tradition of boys wearing blue-and-white sailor suits also persists in many areas. First Communion clothes are worn again for going to church on Sunday and for ceremonial occasions, especially weddings.

The bride wore black

White wedding dresses are generally popular. The bride wears a veil or a mantilla and flowers in her hair. Bridegrooms wear a formal suit. However, some

First communion is a very special day—a chance to dress like a grown-up for the first time.

brides are reviving the custom of marrying in a black lace or silk gown and a black mantilla. This symbolizes faithfulness until death. In Andalusia, frilled, flamenco-style wedding dresses are also popular.

Black is also the color of mourning. Older widows who do not remarry traditionally wear black for the rest of their lives, especially in rural districts. The mantilla is a very important item, especially in southern Spain. Even younger, fashion-conscious women might wear a black lace mantilla for funerals and for other church ceremonies.

Weddings are formal occasions. People whose job involves wearing a uniform often dress in this for the ceremony.

Dressed in their best

At major festivals such as the Seville *feria*, you can see couples on horseback. The women ride sidesaddle behind their partner. They wear the traditional flounced dress with a mantilla, a comb, and an embroidered silk shawl, while the men wear *caballero* costume.

Black work embroidery

The ancient Spanish technique of black stitchery on white fabric was taken to England by Catherine of Aragon, first wife of Henry VIII. She was a skilled embroiderer. It was known as poor man's lace because it looked like lace from a distance. Traditionally, Spanish brides embroidered their groom's wedding shirt.

Fashion for the Boys

Spain is still a fairly conservative society. What men wear reflects their social status and their personality. They are expected to dress appropriately for work and for going out.

The macho male

Traditionally, Spanish men are not great shoppers. Most men's clothes are still bought by their wives or mothers. However, they like to look good. In the last 10 years, younger men have become much more fashion conscious. Menswear design is big business. Young Spanish designers compete alongside Italian labels such as Hugo Boss and Armani.

The Cordobés hat

This wide-brimmed, flat-crowned hat is the symbol of Spain. It comes, as its name suggests, from Córdoba in Andalusia. It is so famous, there is a song about it, which includes the words: "There is none other as pure and Spanish, nor one that equals it in beauty because the sun's rays baptized its charm."

The famous Cordobés hat was designed to give shade from the fierce Andalusian sun.

Provocative designers such as David Delfin offer unconventional garments, such as jackets with one short and one long sleeve or necklines that look like a noose. Not many men would dare to wear these, but they draw attention to Spain's growing fashion industry.

Formal wear

City dwellers and businessmen are well turned out in dark suits, white shirts, and stylish shoes. Linen suits in beige, cream, or black replace the fine wool in summer. For eating out or going to a concert, men dress very formally. They are hardly ever seen without a tie.

Fashion has not yet arrived in rural areas. Here formal wear for men is a white shirt and black pants, often with a black vest. Hats are worn for church.

The next generation

Young Spaniards are as eager to wear American jeans and sneakers as anyone in Europe. However, most teenagers have a formal suit for Sunday, and little brothers often have a mini-version.

Like all teenagers, Spanish youngsters love American-style jeans, hoodies, and sneakers.

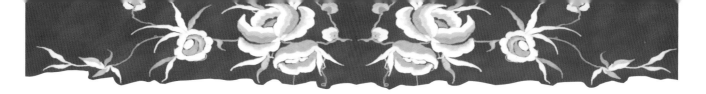

Women's Fashions

Historically, Spain has not been greatly influenced by international fashion trends, and Spanish women used to be considered old-fashioned in their dress. The standard of living in Spain was not high, and not many women worked outside the home. They did not need and could not afford expensive clothing. All this has changed in the last few years.

Stylish girls

Spanish fashion is still conservative but always stylish. Silk and fine-wool tailored suits are very popular, usually in dark or muted colors. Knee-length

Cutting-edge Spanish fashion from Agatha Ruiz de la Prada. One of the designs gives a new look to flamenco flounces.

skirts are more popular than pants, worn with silk blouses and high heels. For evening wear, however, women like clinging stretch fabrics that show off their trim figures.

Real revolution

Cristóbal Balenciaga, Spain's most famous fashion designer, found inspiration in traditional styles and colors. The new generation of Spanish designers do the same, although they also follow international trends. Not many of them are famous yet outside Spain, but Spanish women prefer their clothes. The flamenco-style dress has been given a modern makeover. Whole fashion shows are devoted to this very Spanish style.

Younger women prefer stylish separates from chain stores such as Zara and Mango. They are hugely popular and now export Spanish clothing worldwide.

For formal occasions and going to church, many women still wear a plain black dress and cover their hair with a mantilla.

The mantilla

The mantilla is a lace veil and the symbol of Spanish womanhood. Almost always black or white, it is worn over a long comb made of ivory or tortoiseshell. This is pinned into the hair, and the mantilla is arranged so that it falls in folds over the neck and shoulders.

The mantilla adds an air of dignity to whatever outfit it is worn with.

Uniform Style

In the Franco era, uniforms were very formal. The government wanted their officials to be easily recognizable. More recently, uniforms have become more relaxed.

Police

Spain has three types of police. They all wear approximately the same uniform but in different colors. They wear short-sleeved shirts, jackets in winter, pants, and caps. The Guardia Civil (National Guard), who look after rural areas, wear olive green. Their distinctive shovel-shaped hat has been replaced by a cap with a flat circular top and a visor (similar

This rare photo, from about 1900, shows the original Guardia Civil uniform and hat.

to the French kepi) for everyday duties. The Policia Nacional (National Police) wear white shirts and black pants, and the local police wear blue. In the Basque country, the police uniform is similar to the traditional costume. Basque police wear a white shirt, black pants, and the famous red beret.

The armed services

Military uniforms for active service are also much simpler than they used to be. The army wears olive green blouson jackets, pants, shirts, ties, and black shoes and socks. The air force wears the same in blue, and the navy wears dark blue and white. However, some of the dress uniforms from the period before the Spanish Civil War (1936–1939) have been revived recently. These are much more elaborate, especially the hats.

Simplicity at school

There are no school uniforms in Spain. Younger children used to wear smocks or aprons over their ordinary clothes, but these are now seen only in country areas.

These ceremonial uniforms are very different from those worn on active service!

An unofficial army

During the Spanish Civil War, people from all countries fought in International Brigades. The Abraham Lincoln Brigade had recruits from all over the United States. Because it was illegal to fight in a foreign war, they bought uniforms in army surplus stores and made their own way to Spain as tourists.

Dressing for Leisure

The Spanish like to look stylish, even in casual clothing. However hot it is, they usually wear tailored clothes and rarely look sloppy.

Cotton and linen suits are popular in khaki, cream, or black. Denim jeans are usually worn clean and pressed. Women opt for sleeveless linen dresses or dresses and separates in stretch fabrics, usually with high-heeled sandals.

Holiday dress code

No one wears shorts, torn or cutoff jeans, or skimpy T-shirts in the city. Churches and sometimes restaurants have signs outside asking people to dress properly. Beach clothes are especially frowned on. The vacation island of Ibiza has its own style of casual clothing, in fine white linen.

Espadrilles

These rope-soled canvas sandals come from Catalonia, where they were worn by peasants. The name comes from esparto, a kind of wiry grass originally used for the soles. Famous shoe designer Manolo Blahnik became interested in shoes when he watched his mother make espadrilles.

Farmers and fishermen wore espadrilles because they are light on the feet and they dry out quickly if they get wet.

Night owls

Spaniards like to stay up late. Restaurants serve dinner until midnight, and clubs stay open all night in summer. The evening begins with the paseo. People put on their best clothes and stroll around the streets. They meet their friends, play with their children, eat ice cream, and drink coffee.

Sports

The Spanish soccer team plays in red shirts with a yellow shoulder stripe, blue shorts, and blue socks. Supporters often wear team shirts when they go to matches.

Bullfighting is still popular in Spain. Going to the bullring is a special occasion for which people dress up. The matador has a very elaborate traditional costume known as the "suit of lights" because of its shiny sequins.

Although many people consider bullfighting cruel, it is a kind of theatrical display, in which costume plays a major part.

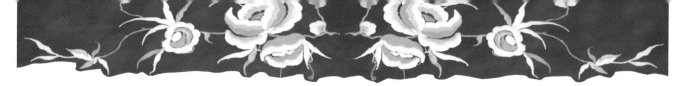

Finishing Touches

Spain is especially famous for its high-quality leather accessories, including belts, boots and shoes, handbags, and wallets. The softest leather is used to make gloves. Traditional accessories, such as fans and mantillas, are not only made for tourists. Modern city-dwelling Spaniards also wear them with modern fashion outfits on occasion.

Fans and shawls

Fans come in all kinds of material, from lace to paper. They can be plain or painted with flowers and historical scenes. Another very typical item is the silk shawl. These are triangular in shape and have a long fringe. The best are hand-embroidered with brightly colored flowers.

Jewelry

The Andalusian gypsies traditionally wore large hoop earrings made of gold. These are still worn by many Spanish

Girls at the Seville fiesta, wearing traditional hoop earrings. The girl on the left holds castanets, with which she will make a rhythmic clicking sound to accompany her dancing.

women along with tiny gold crucifixes on chains, given as Confirmation gifts. Most women also have a string or two of imitation pearls, traditionally made on the island of Mallorca.

Hairstyles and hats

Traditionally, Spanish men had mustaches, but today most are clean shaven and wear their black hair short. Women tend to wear their hair long and loose or swept up and pinned with combs. These are made of carved tortoiseshell or ivory and are also worn with the mantilla.

Spanish men look very dashing in the traditional Cordobés hat (see page 18) or the deeper-crowned Sevillano. Men usually wear black or gray hats, but Andalusian women also wear them, in bright red.

The language of fans

Women used fans to give secret messages. Hiding the eyes behind an open fan meant "I love you." Opening and closing the fan quickly several times meant "I am jealous." Fanning slowly meant "I am married," while pressing a half-open fan to the lips meant "You may kiss me."

Spanish women used to have fans of every fabric and color to match each of their outfits.

Spain and the World

Because of its isolated position, modern Spain has not been greatly influenced by other cultures. American casual style, however, is as popular here as everywhere else in Europe. Immigration from North Africa is now bringing Muslim culture back to Spain after 400 years. Other countries love Spain's romantic gypsy image and its dashing, colorful costumes.

Swinging style

In Britain and America in the 1950s, Spanish style was the new fashion. Short bolero jackets and tight-fitting "toreador pants" for women were all the rage. Modern designers use features such as high-waisted pants and fringed jackets rather than flounces and ruffles. They also borrow the rich jewel colors Spaniards love—purple, pink, and emerald green.

Although the dress is different, this Mexican costume shows many Spanish influences—the embroidered flowers, the fan, the flowers in the hair.

It is strange to see the costume of 19th-century Spain on the plains of South America today.

Latin America

Spanish style is still visible all over Central and South America, the former territories of the Spanish Empire. The gaucho (cowboy) costume is just like the Spanish riding outfit. It has a short jacket, calf-length pants, and a hat like the Cordobés. Tight-fitting flamenco-style dresses, with frills and flounces, are seen all over South America. This is based on the *maja* style of the 18th century. Latin American brides often wear black lace wedding dresses and mantillas.

Native American weaving

When the Spanish introduced sheep to America, some indigenous tribes became shepherds. They used the wool to weave clothing and decorative textiles. The patterns and color schemes are similar to Moorish originals.

Cristóbal Balenciaga

From the 1930s to the 1960s, Balenciaga was the most famous designer in the world. He inspired other designers such as Hubert de Givenchy, Emanuel Ungaro, and Andre Courrèges. The Spanish royal family and, later, Jackie Kennedy wore his clothes. Although he was inspired by traditional Spanish clothing, his most famous creation was the "sack dress," which had no shape at all.

Glossary

beret A soft, round, brimless cap, usually made of felted wool.

black work An embroidery technique involving abstract designs worked in tiny black stitches on white fabric.

bolero A very short jacket worn by men and women.

brocade A richly decorative woven fabric.

Burgundians Rulers of the province of eastern France who were at the height of their power during the medieval period.

caballero The dress style of the horsemen of Andalusia.

chivalry A code of honor that governed the behavior of medieval knights.

Crusades A series of military expeditions made by European Christians in the 11th to 13th centuries to retake areas of the Middle East captured by Muslim forces.

Cuban heel A broad heel of medium height.

farthingale A wire-framed underskirt worn to make the skirt stick out from the waist.

feria A public festival or holiday.

flamenco The music and dance of Andalusia.

gabardine A hardy wool or cotton fabric used to make suits, overcoats, pants, and other garments.

gaucho A South American cowboy.

hose Close-fitting stockings.

Ibiza An island in the Mediterranean belonging to Spain.

Islam The religion of Muslims, founded in the seventh century and based on the teachings of Muhammad.

kepi A high-crowned cap with a flat, circular top and a visor.

linen A fine woven fabric made from the flax plant.

macho Having exaggerated masculine qualities.

mantilla A lace veil or small shawl that covers the head and shoulders.

matador The main bullfighter, whose job it is to kill the bull.

Meseta A plateau in central Spain.

Moors Muslims from North Africa of mixed Arab and Berber descent.

Muslim A follower of Islam.

muslin Very fine, almost transparent cotton fabric.

nazareno A member of a religious brotherhood. *Nazarene* (someone from Nazareth) was an old word for "Christian."

penitentes Penitents, or people seeking forgiveness for their sins.

Roman Catholicism A Christian Church that has a pope as its head and is administered from the Vatican City in Rome.

ruff A cartwheel-shaped starched collar that ties around the neck.

tooled Having a design pressed or stamped into a material, such as leather, by means of a hand tool.

toreador A foreign word for *matador*, not used in Spain.

turban A head covering made by winding a long strip of cloth around the head.

vestments Ceremonial clothing worn by priests.

Further Information

Books

Champion, Neil. *Countries of the World: Spain*. Chelsea House Publishers, 2006.

Harris, Nathaniel. *Nations of the World: Spain*. Raintree, 2004.

Parker, Edward. *The Changing Face of Spain*. Raintree, 2003.

Tierney, Tom. *Italian and Spanish Fashion Designers: Paper Dolls*. Dover, 2005.

Tierney, Tom. *Spanish and Moorish Fashions*. Dover, 2003.

Web sites

www.spain.info
A Web site containing general information about Spanish life and culture aimed at tourists.

www.fashionfromspain.com
A Web site devoted to current Spanish fashion.

www.flamenco-world.com
An online magazine focusing on the world of flamenco.

www.worldweddingtraditions.com
A Web site looking at wedding traditions around the world, including Spain.

www.costume.org
General costume information.

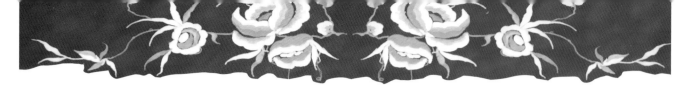

Index